❖ **Why They Became Famous** ❖

# ALBERT SCHWEITZER

❖ **Why They Became Famous** ❖

# ALBERT SCHWEITZER

**Gabriella Cremaschi**

**Translated by Stephen Thorne**

**Illustrated by Gianni Renna**

**Silver Burdett Company**

2877

**Library of Congress Cataloging in Publication Data**

Cremaschi, Gabriella, 1952–
  Albert Schweitzer.

  (Why they became famous)
  Translation of: Perchè sono diventati famosi,
Albert Schweitzer.
  Summary: Traces the life of the humanitarian who
gave up a comfortable academic existence to become a
missionary doctor in the jungles of Gabon.
    1. Schweitzer, Albert, 1875–1965 — Juvenile literature.
2. Missionaries, Medical — Gabon — Biography — Juvenile
literature. 3. Missions, Medical — Gabon — Lambarene —
Juvenile literature. [1. Schweitzer, Albert, 1875–1965.

  2. Missionaries. 3. Physicians. 4. Missions — Gabon]
I. Title. II. Series.
R722.32.S35C7513   1985     610'.92'4 [B] [92]     84-40404
ISBN 0-382-06986-2
ISBN 0-382-06856-4 (lib. bdg.)

© Fabbri Editori S.p.A., Milan 1982
Translated into English by Stephen Thorne for Silver Burdett Company from
Perché Sono Diventati Famosi: Albert Schweitzer
First published in Italy in 1982 by Fabbri Editori S.p.A., Milan

# CONTENTS

**Page**

# An Unusual Decision

Albert Schweitzer was very tired. It was early evening, and while he walked slowly home he thought over the events of the long day he had just put in. As usual he had risen quite early, shortly before six o'clock. For two hours he practiced the organ and afterwards went over to St. Nicholas' church where he preached every morning. He had spent the rest of his day attending to his duties as rector of the Theological College of Strasbourg University.

There was just no end to his work and responsibilities. He had just published a book on theology called *The Search for the Historical Jesus* and had now begun writing a book about the composer, Bach. Just two days earlier he had been called upon to restore an antique organ in a nearby town, but he still hadn't found time to go over and see just how much work the job would involve.

Schweitzer's life was particularly difficult for him during this period. For some time he had been searching for a way to devote his life to serving others in a more tangible way. He wanted to pursue a career which might enable him to alleviate some of the suffering he saw in the world. He would be turning thirty in a few days and had not yet decided what his new work was to be.

Exhausted, he entered his small apartment and with little interest went through the pile of mail on the table. Just as he was about to toss aside the letters, a green pamphlet caught his attention. It was a small publication that the Society of the Evangelical Mission of Paris issued every month as a report on its activities. As he thumbed through the pamphlet his eye fell upon an article about Gabon, one of the most disease-ridden areas in Africa. The people there had to survive without much medical assistance at all. There were few doctors to be found within a radius of several hundred miles. Many of the natives still died of diseases which were no longer considered fatal in Europe. If just one person were to step forward and courageously offer skills and service, many lives could be saved. Schweitzer felt the book was speaking directly to him.

"Would you go?" it seemed to say. "Would you give up everything you have here to go and be a doctor in Africa?"

Schweitzer thought briefly and then decided he *would* go. He would enroll in the University and study medicine, at the same time trying to raise enough money to fund the expedition.

The next day he told his fiancée, Hélène Bresslau, of his plans. She listened to him intently and, when he had finished, reflected on what he had said for a moment. Then, she spoke.

"I'll wait for you to complete your studies and then go with you."

"But do you realize what that means?" he interrupted. "You will have to leave everything behind—music, studies, family, friends—and you will have to face danger and discomfort. It won't be an easy life. I can't allow you to do this. Besides, what would you do with yourself there?"

"I'll study nursing while you're going to medical school at the University. Then, when we go to Africa I will be able to work at your side!" she announced with a pleased smile.

Schweitzer kept to his rooms for several days afterwards. When he finally emerged he went straight to the post office and mailed a stack of letters. In some of the letters he had told his closer friends about the decision he had made. In others he resigned from the various posts he held at that time. In the days to come he would need to devote as much of his time and energy as was possible to his medical studies.

Soon he began to receive replies from friends and associates. His decision had caused quite a stir in academic and musical circles in both Germany and France. All those who wrote used the same argument in an attempt to persuade him to reverse his decision. It wasn't right they said, that he, of all people, a musical genius, noted philosopher, gifted preacher, and a first-class theologian, should willingly renounce the work which nature had so splendidly equipped him to do. There were other people able to care for the sick in Gabon as well as or even better than he could. He just couldn't do it, went the argument. He should content himself with his preaching, and instead use the proceeds from his concerts and royalties from his publications to support the missions in Africa.

Schweitzer tried to explain to everyone his reasons for abandoning his studies to devote himself to something practical which would yield visible results. His attempts failed, however, and when he realized that it was impossible to convince his friends and colleagues, he stopped trying to explain. Let them think he was a fool. It didn't matter. His mind was made up and he was content with his decision.

Before beginning his medical studies there was still another painful duty he wanted to perform. He had to tell his parents of the decision he had made, and try to win their approval. He returned to his childhood home in Gunsbach, a small village in Alsace, (at the time a part of Germany), where his parents still lived. When he arrived home he immediately told them of his plans and found it difficult to persuade them that the enterprise would not be terribly dangerous. His parents were well aware of the situation in Gabon, and the atrocious conditions in which people were forced to live in that faraway land. However, they both shared the profound love and concern for humanity which had inspired their son's decision. They were also fully aware of how difficult a road he had chosen to follow.

Schweitzer stayed on for a few days' holiday in Gunsbach. He was able to walk, perhaps for the last time, through the streets and meadows which had been the scene of his childhood games and pastimes. As he wandered about he recalled several episodes from his childhood which had, even then, perhaps unconsciously prepared the way for the life of service to others upon which he was about to embark.

Schweitzer's father was a Lutheran pastor in the village of Gunsbach. For the most part the people of the town were very poor. Young Albert had been the only well-dressed boy in the village school. The other boys had felt that he was different from them. Above all else, Albert's shyness had made him quiet and reserved, and so any of the efforts he made to become friendly with his classmates had been ignored. Albert always seemed to stand apart from the others and watch his classmates as they played. No one ever asked him if he wanted to join in. If he wanted to play with them, he would have to do something about it himself.

One day after school a group of Albert's classmates were talking and laughing on their way home. Albert tried to join in their fun, but only managed to anger a boy named George and get on his bad side. George was a tall, hefty boy and not a good person to be at odds with. Since he was bigger than the other children, he was generally looked up to as the leader of the group. He came slowly up to Albert, spitting on his hands.

"Come on, you little wimp!" he shouted.

Albert had never been in a fight before. He realized that George was much stronger than he was, but he summoned up his courage and threw himself at his adversary. The outcome of the fight was uncertain for some time, but with a valiant effort Albert managed to knock George to the ground. An astonished murmur went through the crowd of onlookers. There was no doubt about it, the "wimp" had won!

Albert offered his hand to George with a smile, but the bigger boy refused his help.

"If we had as much to eat in my house as you have in yours," George shouted angrily, "I know I would've half killed you!"

Those words hurt Albert harder than any blow from a fist could have. That day he discovered the existence of poverty.

The Sunday following the fight, Albert had to put on a new overcoat that his parents had given him for his birthday. The tailor had finished it in a great hurry on Saturday evening, and the whole family was eager to see the impression Albert made when he wore it to church. Albert, however, refused to put it on.

"Why not?" asked his father.

"I don't want to, that's all."

"Perhaps you don't like it because it's been made from one of my old coats? Well Albert, you know very well that we aren't rich. We can't afford to buy you a brand new coat."

"No, father, that's not the reason."

"Well, what is it, then?"

"The other boys in the village haven't got nice coats like this."

"Well, at least your reason does you credit. But I can't have the members of my congregation thinking that I can't afford to dress my son properly. Put it on immediately, Albert!"

"No, I won't!"

"Are you refusing to obey your father?"

"Yes."

"You know what I shall be obliged to do, don't you?"

"I'm sorry father, but I'm convinced that I've made the right decision."

That Sunday morning Albert received one of the first really serious punishments of his life. Every Sunday throughout the winter he had to choose between wearing the overcoat and a beating from his father, and each time he chose the beating.

Soon though, his parents realized that the reasons for their son's refusal were rooted in the profound concern he felt for others. They knew that if they cultivated this feeling properly it would bear fruit later in the boy's life. So after

some time, Albert was no longer asked to put on the coat, and his parents tolerated the gossip about them with good grace. It didn't matter if the villagers thought they couldn't afford to dress their son better.

After the fight with George, Albert had gradually managed to become friendly with his schoolmates. After all, he had shown great courage in fighting their leader and had to be accepted into the gang, even if he was a "wimp"! This acceptance marked the beginning of a new and much happier period in Albert's life—a period of games and forays into the surrounding woods. In the early summer, children spent their mornings wandering through the woods hunting for animals and birds.

One day Albert and a friend trooped off into the woods to shoot birds with their sling-shots. It was difficult, so the boys were tense and alert. They had to move carefully to avoid making the least bit of noise which would frighten the birds, and make them fly away. Neither had managed to see anything to shoot at, but at last they caught sight of a whole flock of birds in a large, leafless tree.

It was Albert's turn to shoot, but he had been worrying about whether he could do anything to hurt the birds for some time. He looked at the birds sitting there innocently and unsuspectingly. He didn't really want to kill them, but didn't know how could he explain this to his friend. Nevertheless, he loaded his sling shot and took aim. Just at that moment, the bells in the churches nearby started to chime. Albert heard them and realized it was a signal to him. He clapped his hands and the birds flew off. With this, he turned and ran home.

Later, Schweitzer was reminded every time he heard the bells before Easter of that day when he found he could not kill a bird. He also learned not to fear being laughed at by his schoolmates because he was different.

# A Difficult Period of Preparation

As Schweitzer looked back at Gunsbach from the train that was to take him back to Strasbourg, he reflected on how peaceful and happy his childhood had been. He had certainly been the luckiest child in the village. Compared with the children in Gabon, he had had the childhood of a prince. Such thoughts only served to further convince him that he had made the right decision. Up until now, life had been very good to him and now it was time to do something for those who were not as fortunate.

In his mind, he went over the number of years that it would take before he could start his new work. It would take six years to get his medical degree. Then he would have to spend a year as an intern in a hospital. After that, if he really wanted to be useful in Africa, he would have to specialize in tropical diseases. He would be thirty-eight years old when he would finally be ready to leave!

As soon as he returned to Strasbourg he began his studies at the university there. Many students were astonished to see that one of their number was a man who, until a short while ago, had been the principal of one of the colleges at the university. Nevertheless, Schweitzer was quickly able to win their friendship and trust. His life was much more difficult than theirs, however. Medical studies were difficult for everyone, but Schweitzer had to support himself as well as study. Unlike the other students, he had no family to fall back on who could finance his studies, so these were very difficult years for him. He took courses at the University, and at the same time supported himself by continuing to pursue some of his previous activities.

Now and then he was asked to save an old organ from destruction. After so many years of devotion to this task, he found it very difficult to ignore these requests. He continued to preach at St. Nicholas'. This was very important to him, as it fulfilled a deep spiritual need which the dry, scientific discipline of medical study could certainly never satisfy. Every now and then he was invited to give concerts in various European cities, and of course, he went. Apart from the personal satisfaction it always gave him to play Bach, he could not afford to ignore this means of financial support.

During the six years from 1905 to 1911, he divided his time among medicine, music, and studying. At long last, he took his final examinations in December, 1911. After passing them he spent a year of practice in a Strasbourg hospital as an intern. Then he went to Paris for a few months to study tropical medicine.

He was now a fully qualified doctor. All the papers needed for his departure were ready. After taking the necessary courses, Hélène, too, had taken her examinations and was now a qualified nurse. She had waited for Albert all those years, helping him and offering her support to him during difficult moments.

They were married on June 18, 1911. After their studies were completed, the husband and wife were busy for several months more organizing the shipment of all the supplies they would need in Africa. With the aid of members of the Paris Missionary Society, which had a mission at Lambaréné in Gabon, they drafted a work project which would be started immediately upon the Schweitzers' arrival. Attaching themselves to the existing mission, they would open a hospital to serve the whole region surrounding the mission. The French missionaries already in Gabon assured the Schweitzers that they could depend upon their support. In addition, the missionaries promised that they would build a metal hut as a start to the complete hospital which would follow someday. It was to be in place when Hélène and Albert arrived in Gabon.

The Schweitzers' work would be much easier if a proper building was there, ready and waiting for them. They would then be able to receive their first patients soon after their arrival. In time, the project would grow and other volunteer doctors would be able to join them.

For the moment, however, all these things were only dreams. They had to keep their feet on the ground and set to work acquiring everything needed for at least three years of independent existence in Gabon. This was the minimum amount of time they would have to stay in order to see whether or not their enterprise could be successful.

There was a vast amount of medical equipment that needed to be collected. Then it also had to be carefully packed, and shipped. The Schweitzers spent many days drawing up lists of medicines and equipment, and still more going from shop to shop buying everything. At long last, the packing cases containing all they had collected were sealed and sent to Bordeaux. From there the Schweitzers were to leave for Africa. Many friends had made donations on their behalf. It was thanks to this generosity that the hospital at Lambaréné would be equipped well enough to be fairly independent and have all the surgical instruments needed.

However, now that they were ready to leave, a dark political cloud appeared on the horizon. The great European powers were moving rapidly towards open conflict. It was reasonable to suppose that the fragile relations that existed between the governments of the various countries would soon break down.

What would happen to the Schweitzers if war broke out between France and Germany? They were Germans and Gabon was then a French colony (at that time it was called French Equatorial Africa). If there were open hostilities they would find themselves in an enemy country. Apart from any concerns about their personal safety, what made them most bitter was the great contrast between the aim of their journey to Africa and the situation in their homeland, not to mention throughout the whole of Europe. While they were leaving with a message of peace and goodwill to the world, their native land was moving closer and closer towards causing widespread death and despair.

"The bells of the church in my native village in Alsace had just stopped ringing on Good Friday afternoon in 1913," Schweitzer later wrote, "when the train that was to take us away appeared on the edge of the wood. We got onto the platform of the last carriage and our journey to Africa began. As we waved farewell, between the trees, I saw the bell-tower for perhaps the last time. When would I ever see it

again?...The next day, when Strasbourg cathedral also disappeared from view, we already seemed to be in a foreign land."

In Paris, the Schweitzers met with the members of the Bach Society for the last time. Albert had been one of its founding members in 1906. They listened to a concert given by C.M. Widor, who was a dear friend and teacher of Schweitzer.

When it came time to say farewell, their friends in the Bach Society gave the couple a wedding present—an enormous wooden case containing an upright piano that was very similar to an organ.

"This way you can keep in practice," they said. "So, when you return one day, you can play again in our churches and halls." The piano was lined inside with a layer of zinc to protect it from the termites they would find in Africa.

Later in the afternoon, the Schweitzers left for Bordeaux. Two days after, they boarded the *Europe*, a small shallow-draft ship which would carry them on this leg of their journey from Europe down the coast of West Africa. After many days of sailing, during which the Schweitzers experienced violent storms and the deadly heat of the equatorial sun, the *Europe* put in at a small port on the Ogowe River.

# In Africa at Last

Their journey continued up the Ogowe, the main waterway of the region, in the *Alambe*, a small paddle steamer. The Schweitzers studied the landscape around them, and saw the interior of Africa for the first time. Albert jotted down his first impression of what was to be his new home. "Water and primeval forest...It's as if I'm dreaming. You just can't tell where the water ends and the land begins, everything is like a mirror. The forest is like a huge rampart emitting the most unendurable heat."

Sounding its whistle, the *Alambe* put in at a small port in the interior of the country, which was still an hour from the mission itself.

"There was no one there to meet us," wrote Schweitzer, "but as we were disembarking (it was four o'clock and the sun was still very strong) a long, thin canoe suddenly appeared, paddled by a group of young men who were singing joyously. It shot towards us and circled the steamer so quickly that when it neared the thick

cable tying the steamer to the shore, the white man seated in it just managed to duck and avoid being injured badly. This was Christol, the Protestant missionary, and the paddlers were members of the youngest class in the mission school. Another canoe, filled with pupils in an older class, rushed up behind them carrying another missionary, Ellenberger. The two classes had raced each other, and the younger pupils had won. They were now teasing the older pupils because the winners had the honor of carrying the doctor and his wife, while the losers had to carry the baggage. What wonderful young lads they were! We were a little thrown at first because each canoe was carved from a single tree-trunk and threatened to overturn at the slightest movement. The crew paddled standing up, which didn't improve stability either, while plying the water with long paddles and chanting in quick rhythm. If one of them had missed a stroke we could all have been thrown head over heels. After half an hour or so we were no longer afraid, and admired the splendid scenery. The crew raced the steamer which had taken to the river again and we narrowly avoided capsizing a small canoe containing three natives who cursed us in an extremely difficult guttural dialect."

After about an hour, the Schweitzers caught sight of some white houses nestled on three low hills near the banks of a creek which led off the main river. These were the bungalows of the Paris Missionary Society. Schweitzer was to build his hospital near them. When the canoe had put in at the small landing, they were met by a cheering crowd who had been waiting on the banks for them to arrive. As the Schweitzers set foot on land they were garlanded with flowers and palm branches, and obliged to shake dozens upon dozens of hands. The crowd followed them up the hill and to the house where they were to live.

It was very late when the Schweitzers took a last look at their new country from the window of the house. From the dense forest, natural sounds mingled with the rhythm of the drum beats that announced the arrival of the white doctor.

At first light the next day, the Schweitzers hurried from their home, anxious to see the hospital building which the missionaries had promised them. Schweitzer was stunned.

"Why, there's nothing here!"

"Unfortunately," explained Father Christol, "we haven't been able to persuade the natives to work for us lately. This is the only season during which they can make a little money by cutting precious wood in the forest."

"We'll soon make up for lost time," they declared, trying to cheer themselves up.

Their conversation was soon interrupted by the sound of approaching voices. A whole fleet of overloaded canoes was coming down the river, and a crowd of natives was climbing up the hill towards them. Many were limping and others were being carried. Schweitzer was furious when he realized that they had all come to see him.

"No, it can't be possible! I said I would only see urgent cases for the first three weeks. The crates of medicine haven't arrived, and I can't examine patients out of doors with no shelter whatsoever."

But he was forced to change his mind. They were all urgent cases, and he had to administer cursory treatment just to keep some of them alive. Leprosy, malaria, sleeping sickness, yellow fever, tropical sores, pneumonia and hernias—the list of illnesses was endless and he couldn't even speak a word of their language. However, the expressions on his patients' faces said it all—the white doctor had to help them.

The Schweitzers worked side-by-side all day long. They quickly separated the contagious cases from the others, and treated everyone with the supplies and medicines they had. When night fell they were obliged to abandon their work, but the line of patients was still as long as it had been in the morning. They were tired out, but didn't sleep much that night.

"At least we've got a bed," Albert said to his wife, "which is more than those poor souls have, curled up on the ground waiting for morning and being attacked by mosquitoes. They might get malaria, in addition to the other diseases they are suffering from. No, we can't go on like this. The boat carrying the rest of our things

won't be arriving here for another ten days, but we'll have to do something in the meantime."

"The only unused building at the mission is that old brokendown chicken coop at the edge of the clearing," said Hélène. "We could use that."

"What! Have you seen the condition of it? It's filthy. It has no floor and the roof has fallen in."

"Yes, I know, but at the moment we haven't got the time or the materials to build anything else. We can clean it up with lime and find something to use to patch up the holes in the roof."

Even though it was a desperate measure, it was the only way they could have a shelter to work in. So, early the next day, they became builders. They covered over the dirt with lime, whitewashed the walls, and filled in the holes in the walls and roof. A single bed they had found in the mission was to serve as a makeshift operating table, and some old shelves that were on the wall became a cabinet for the medical instruments.

The next ten days were a nightmare for the Schweitzers. All the medicines they had brought with them from Europe were quickly used up, while the number of sick, some in very serious condition, grew before their weary eyes. Schweitzer learned later that the local witch-doctors had sent all their most desperate cases to him for treatment. They were attempting to discourage him, and at the same time to sow the seeds of distrust in the minds of the Africans. Many patients did die in those early days. Often, the Schweitzers had to bury the bodies themselves, for the local people were so frightened of death that they would abandon the body of a relative rather than touch a corpse.

After ten nightmarish days and nights of desperate waiting, a loud whistle finally announced the arrival of the steamer.

"It was the whistle of resurrection," wrote Schweitzer. "The boat carrying my packing cases was arriving, and our long nightmare was over."

It took three days to carry everything up the hill from the river to the mission. Cabinets had to be built to hold all the medicines and surgical instruments. Life would now be somewhat easier at Lambaréné. Several days later Schweitzer performed his first major operation—a strangulated hernia that was threatening to develop into peritonitis. When the patient was carried outside and those waiting could see he was well, there was a shout of joyful thanks. The Africans had discovered that his was a healing knife, not a deadly one.

# Building the Hospital

However, the joy the Schweitzers experienced at receiving the seventy packing cases was quickly overshadowed by other enormous problems which were caused by the lack of a suitable hospital building. These problems needed to be solved urgently.

"All my work," wrote Schweitzer in his memoirs, "is hindered by the fact that only a very small amount of medicine can be kept in the chicken coop. To treat almost every patient I have to walk across the clearing to my house and weigh out or prepare everything there. This process is very tiring and time-consuming. When can we ever get down seriously to building a hospital? Will we ever manage to finish the job before the rains come? What will we do if it isn't ready? The chicken coop is too hot to work in. New patients are arriving all the time, and my stock of

medicines is going down rapidly—the quinine, aspirin, potassium bromide, phenyl salicylate, and gallate of bismuth are almost finished...three or four months may pass before new supplies arrive from Europe."

Schweitzer soon managed to provide his hospital with a better building. First, they had to fell part of the forest to make a shady, well-ventilated site for the hospital. This took a great deal of money, but above all, it required an enormous amount of labor. It was difficult to persuade the local people to work. But by working hard themselves they set a good example for the Africans, and so Schweitzer and his friends managed to complete the first stage fairly quickly.

However, on the very day on which they had decided they would begin work on the new hut, Schweitzer was called away to treat a seriously ill nun at a mission which was located several days' journey away.

When he was at last able to return, he found a wonderful surprise waiting for him. The metal hut had already been erected! The surprise had been prepared for him by the missionaries, aided by the relatives of patients in the hospital, and supervised by an African named Joseph. Schweitzer had cured him and he had decided to stay on at Lambaréné to help the doctor who had helped him.

29

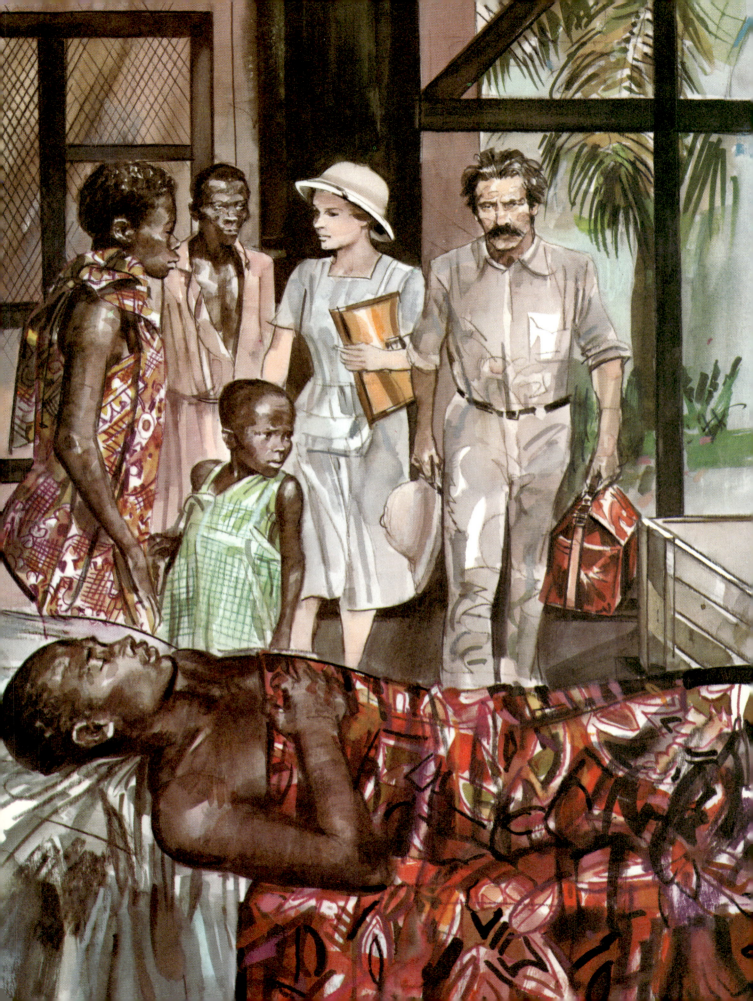

There were two rooms in the hut. The floors were made of cement, and the walls were lined with rows of wooden shelves which held all the hospital's medical equipment.

Other improvements were soon to follow. Several other huts were built to house other units of the hospital. Eventually, Lambaréné had a hospital with two large wards, (one of which was reserved for infectious cases), a medicine storeroom, an examining room, an operating room, and even a waiting room. There were huts surrounding the hospital which were used as accommodations for the relatives of patients who had come from a long distance. The beds were made from tree trunks and vines were used to support bedding.

It could now be said that there was a real hospital at Lambaréné. Patients had their own comfortable beds under which they could keep their food and cooking utensils. Since the hospital couldn't provide food for all the patients, it had been agreed that they should bring enough food with them to last them during their stay in the hospital. Moreover, patients often came great distances to the hospital accompanied by relatives so there were often three or four times the number of patients living outside the hospital as inside it. The only way to ensure that there was sufficient food for all had been for each family to look after itself and its sick. In practice, however, this principle did not always work. Families often came to Lambaréné with little or no food, or the patients had to stay longer than expected and their food ran out. At these times the Schweitzers had to become cooks, too. Neither the mission nor the hospital could afford to employ someone to cook meals, and besides, in Gabon there was hardly a surplus of people looking for work!

After some time had passed, the Schweitzers managed, with the help of the missionaries, to clear some ground for a vegetable garden. It would be a great boost to the hospital's meager financial resources.

Fortunately, there wasn't time enough for the discomforts they suffered to get them down. Every improvement at the hospital also increased its fame, and the hospital at Lambaréné with its white doctor and his magic, healing knife was the only topic of conversation for miles around. Of course, the reputation of the hospital only meant that more and more people hurried there with the hope of being cured by Schweitzer.

It was evident that the Schweitzers had earned the trust and admiration of the Africans and this was enough compensation for the difficult time they were having in keeping the hospital going. Joseph was a great help and comfort to them. The fact that he knew some French simplified their language problems with the patients.

# The Consequences of War

Early in 1914, letters started arriving by steamer at Lambaréné every month containing disturbing news of the situation in Europe. The major powers were rearming quickly and their borders were crowded with artillery and marching armies. War was approaching rapidly.

"If there is a war," wrote Schweitzer during that period, "the forests of Gabon will be a paradise compared with Europe. Out here, killing is a matter between two men, whereas in a European war the carnage will be modern and automatic. It will happen on such a scale that all other wars in the history of man will seem puny and antiquated."

Unfortunately, his predictions were to prove correct. For some time, the Schweitzers had been coming to terms with the fact that their position in Gabon would be extremely delicate if a war broke out. It was a French colony and as Germans they would suddenly find themselves in an enemy country. They might even be deported. The authorities would hesitate to close the hospital if it was seen to be running extremely well, so they began building again and in a short time had erected two new huts. How could the authorities ever have the heart to send all the sick patients back to their homes in the forest?

One day, Schweitzer sent Joseph down to the steamer with some medicine for its captain who, in turn, was to send a sick native up to the hospital whom he had brought with him from a town on the coast. Joseph returned with the medicine still in his hand, and a message from the captain. "War has broken out in Europe, and I have orders to put the steamer at the disposal of the authorities. As a result, I have no idea when we shall ever see each other again."

That very afternoon Schweitzer was visited by a French officer accompanied by a squad of armed Africans. He explained the situation: Since Schweitzer was an enemy citizen, the authorities had decided to suspend all his activities for the time being. From now on, the military authorities in Gabon had decreed, Schweitzer and his wife could have no further contact of any kind with French citizens, whether they be white or black. While waiting for further orders, they would have to remain prisoners under armed guard.

With a heavy heart, Schweitzer tried to think of a way of breaking the news to his patients. He decided to call a general assembly and calmly explain the situation which these latest moves on the part of the authorities had created.

The patients were quickly gathered together in the clearing in front of the hospital, and with a quivering voice, Schweitzer broke the news to them—

"You must return to your homes. I can no longer do anything for you."

Even before he finished speaking the patients turned towards the guards and began shouting and spitting on them. The guards were beginning to level their rifles at the crowd, when Schweitzer, Hélène, and Joseph intervened and were able to prevent the worst from happening.

The hospital buildings were closed and government seals were placed on the doors. The forest drums were busy that night, informing everyone in the jungle that a war had started, the hospital had been closed, and the white doctor had been taken prisoner.

The next day, many of the natives, who had been cured by Schweitzer at one time or another, appeared at the hospital. They asked with bewilderment if the news they had heard was true.

"You have always told us that the white man loves Christ," a woman pointed out, "and that Christ taught love. Why, then, do white men make war on each other?"

The doctor was silent—he had no idea how to answer her. One old man, the chief of the Pahouin group, simply could not understand why the war had broken out.

"The white men shoot each other?" he asked.

"Yes, unfortunately," Schweitzer answered gravely.

"Will many die?"

"I'm afraid so."

The old man, a member of a cannibal group, shook his head.

"Why don't the white men get together and discuss their differences, so that the war can be ended? You have told us that Europeans do not eat their enemies, so that means they kill out of cruelty. I thought the Europeans were better than that."

Once again Schweitzer had no idea how to answer. He, too, thought that the war was motivated only by cruelty and that it would have been better if the heads of all the states involved had gotten together around a table and sorted out the problems which divided them, rather than causing so much death and destruction.

It was strange being there with the hospital closed. The Schweitzers couldn't get over how much free time they had—the days, which until a short time ago had never been long enough, now passed very slowly indeed. Little by little, the

restrictions were relaxed and serious cases were allowed to be treated. Later Schweitzer learned that friends in Paris had talked to the authorities.

Christmas was a sad affair that year, but the Schweitzers decided to celebrate in just the same way as they had in other years. Hélène made palm wreaths and decorated the walls of the house, trying her best to create a festive atmosphere for the occasion.

On Christmas Eve they lit the candles. Albert sat down at the piano and tried to recreate some of the feeling of peace and happiness that Christmas should have whenever and wherever it is celebrated. But it was difficult to dispel the gloom that had settled on the people of Lambaréné. Despite the fact that they were thousands of miles away over the sea, the war had made its presence felt in their forgotten corner of the jungle. Suddenly, Albert got up from the piano and blew out the candles that were only half burned down.

"Why did you do that?" asked his wife.

"We can use them for another year. I don't think we'll be able to get any more before next Christmas."

"It won't be just a problem of candles," Hélène reminded him. "We've only got a few drops of medicine left, and who knows how long it will be before new supplies arrive?"

The war had made communication with Europe very difficult. The new supplies of food and medicine which should have arrived during that period were held up in Bordeaux. They were sitting at the dock waiting for a ship that was authorized to come to Africa. The Schweitzers were even without mail and had received little news of their families for a long time. What little news they did get was certainly not very reassuring.

During that long and unhappy period, Schweitzer continued writing a book he had started in Europe before coming to Africa. His mind was kept busy with his study of the mysticism of St. Paul and this work plus his work on a book about the philosophy of civilization took his mind off the war.

Shortly after that sad Christmas, even the people of Gabon were called to arms by the French army. As a French colony, Gabon and its inhabitants were obliged to defend the motherland across the sea. Schweitzer went down to the landing to see off some of the local people. Those poor young men were going off to a war which they knew nothing about, to defend a country that was not their own. Many of them would die defending their own oppressors.

# Farewell to Lambaréné

Schweitzer stood on the banks of the River Ogowe waiting for the steamer to leave that was carrying away the conscripts.

"Who are the real savages?" he asked himself. "These men who live in the forest and kill out of necessity, or those who have organized a pointless massacre in the very heart of Europe?"

Deeply moved by what he had seen on the river bank, he wrote the following in his diary that evening:

"The crowd had dispersed, but there was still an old woman crouched on the river's edge, weeping silently after watching her son leave for the war. I took her hand and tried to console her, but she continued crying as if I hadn't even spoken. Then, overcome with sadness myself, I started crying beside that old woman on the river bank."

Shortly after the departure of the conscripts, precise instructions were finally received from Europe—all German citizens in Gabon were to be considered prisoners of war, and were to be deported to France.

Schweitzer and his wife were forced to leave Lambaréné under armed guard. They were treated as if they were two dangerous enemies seeking the first opportunity to commit some outrage against the people of Gabon. A huge crowd came to the landing to see them off. It was not easy for those people who had already been cured by the doctor, and even harder for those waiting to be cured by him, to understand why he had to leave because of a war so far away. It was harder still for them to understand why he was being escorted under armed guard like a criminal.

Just before going on board, Schweitzer saw a pair of brilliantly colored poisonous snakes curled up in the grass. There were some children playing a short distance away, completely unaware of the danger lurking nearby. He asked for a rifle and shot the snakes. The episode remained in his mind long afterwards—he was leaving the people of Lambaréné like those two children, defenseless and surrounded by great danger. That day he promised that, at whatever cost, he would return to Lambaréné.

The long journey to Europe was a painful one for the Schweitzers. During their four years in the steamy African climate, they had both suffered with malaria and were beginning to feel the effects of all their strenuous efforts over the years. The only comfort on that long, long voyage would have been the possibility of playing music, to forget their problems and suffering for awhile and find fresh energy to face the unknown destiny that awaited them in Europe.

Of course, there was no piano on board, but Schweitzer devised a way of taking refuge in music just the same. He made the lid of a trunk serve as a keyboard and he moved his feet as if they were sounding the pedals of an organ. In this way, he learned a number of works by Bach which he had never played before.

When they reached Bordeaux, they were sent to a prisoner-of-war camp at Garaison in the Pyrenees. The prisoners were housed in a crumbling monastery. Harsh living conditions and overcrowding led to many health problems for the internees.

Even though he was one of the few doctors in the camp, Schweitzer had been ordered by the authorities not to practice medicine. However, the official doctor was very old and in a short time found himself unable to cope with all the work that was piling up. In addition, the extremely poor sanitary conditions of the camp were increasing the danger of infection and causing more and more prisoners to become ill. It was not long, then, before the doctor came to Schweitzer and asked for his help.

He assigned Dr. Schweitzer to be quartered in his own office. "This way you can be a doctor again," he happily told Schweitzer. Later Schweitzer was able to write that although his stay in the camp had been disastrous as far as his health was concerned, it had been a very positive experience for him from an educational point of view.

"I needed no books to learn from in that place. I fully exploited the fact that, to my great fortune, I was surrounded by men who were experts in architecture, finance, industrial organization, agriculture, furnace construction, and other subjects whose usefulness I was able to appreciate much later."

At Garaison, the Schweitzers realized how well-known they had become in Europe. When news was received of their arrival, the inmates of the camp came to salute the great organist who had abandoned a brilliant career in music to go and serve the people of Africa.

In the spring of that year the Schweitzers were transferred to Saint-Rémy-de-Provence where there was a camp housing only Alsatians. It was rather like being back home, and they met many old acquaintances in the camp.

At last, the great news arrived—as a result of an exchange of prisoners between Germany and France, the inmates of Saint-Rémy-de-Provence were to be liberated. The Schweitzers were sent back to Alsace through Switzerland. An armistice was finally concluded on November 11, 1918, and with the later agreement between France and Germany, Alsace became part of France again.

Two months later Hélène gave birth to a baby daughter, Rhena. For a long while, the Schweitzers devoted all their energies to regaining their health, which had been so cruelly tested in first Africa and then during the year they had spent in the prison camp. Much to their joy and surprise they discovered that they had many friends in Europe, and that many people were anxious to help them. Albert soon found a job and was determined to return to Lambaréné as soon as he could. He traveled throughout Europe giving lectures at the universities and to learned societies that invited him to speak. To all of them he spoke of the hospital in the jungle, the desperate need for medicine in Gabon, and from all he received help, encouragement, and support.

Only one thing was needed to rebuild his shattered health and crown his new-found happiness—the possibility of giving an organ concert of Bach's music. He

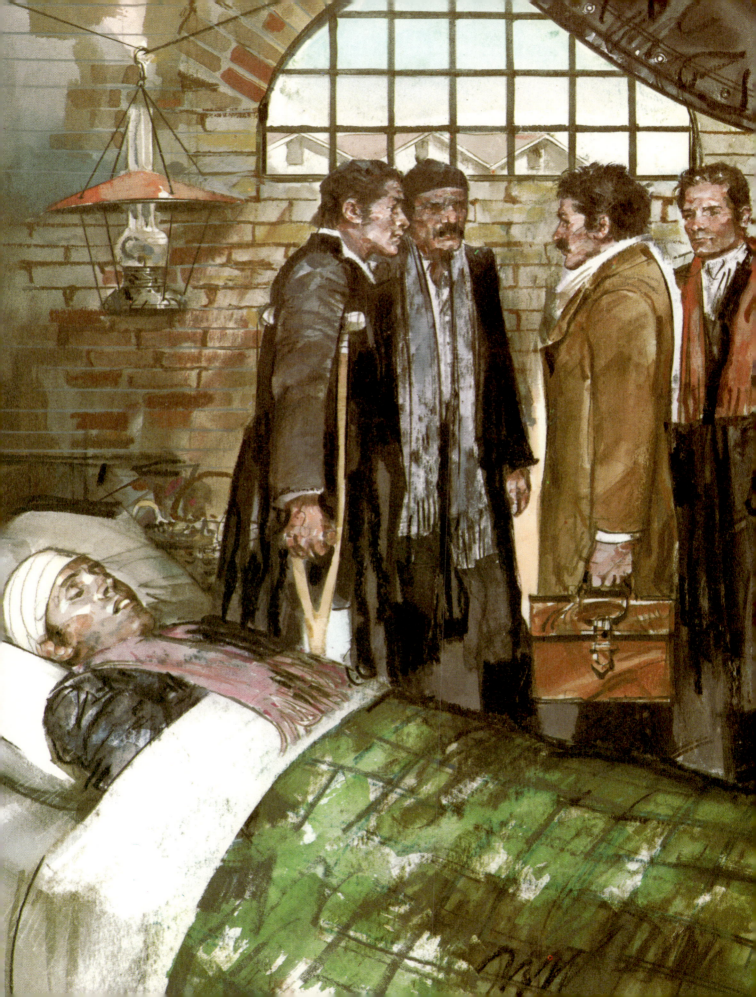

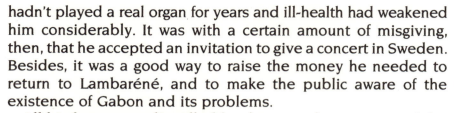

hadn't played a real organ for years and ill-health had weakened him considerably. It was with a certain amount of misgiving, then, that he accepted an invitation to give a concert in Sweden. Besides, it was a good way to raise the money he needed to return to Lambaréné, and to make the public aware of the existence of Gabon and its problems.

All his fears were dispelled by the marvelous success of the first concert. After the audience heard him speak at the end of the concert, they didn't know who to applaud—the great organist or the doctor and his wonderful achievements in Africa.

As a result of these concerts and lectures, an association called "The Friends of Lambaréné" was founded to raise the funds needed to free what everyone now called "the hospital in the jungle" from debt, and allow its doctor to return to the sick people of Gabon.

In the spring of 1923 the plan to return to Gabon took on more definite shape. Schweitzer went back to school again in order to specialize in obstetrics and dentistry. He began his travels again to gather what was needed to get the hospital going once more.

Along with many other gifts, the "Friends" presented the hospital with a large, prefabricated hut which would be the basis for a new, enlarged hospital. Now, it was just a matter of making the final preparations for a return to Africa.

# The White Doctor Returns

On February 21, 1924, at Bordeaux, Schweitzer boarded the steamship that was to take him back to Africa. He was accompanied by a young French medical student, Noel Gillespie, who had offered to stay with him for awhile in Africa. Hélène would rejoin him in Africa when their little daughter was a bit older.

The canoes carrying the two doctors put into the landing at Lambaréné just before Easter, and hundreds of people were waiting on the banks to welcome back the white doctor. As soon as he had disembarked, Schweitzer glanced towards the top of the hill where the hospital was situated. The sight that greeted him made his heart sink. The clearing in the jungle, which had cost him so much effort only a few years before, had been reclaimed by the jungle, and the huts, now roofless, were full of vegetation. Schweitzer turned to the missionaries who had been waiting for his reaction.

"We'll have to start all over again," they said, simply.

The jungle drums beat out the good news that night—the white doctor had returned.

Once again, he had to roll up his sleeves and try to put the huts in order as quickly as possible, because the hospital had to get back into full swing quickly. As had happened in 1913, it was impossible to separate urgent cases from ordinary ones—all the potential patients crowding the hill at Lambaréné were urgent cases. In order to save at least some of them, the doctor needed a quiet place where he could examine them properly.

This time, however, the start of his work was marred by an incident. He was awakened during the night by a groaning sound coming from outside his front door. An old African, who had probably been abandoned by his relatives, was lying helpless outside the hut. Schweitzer watched through the night, but by the morning he was dead. As he was carrying out the body, a young girl started shouting and ran off towards the mission.

"Why do you allow the leopard-men to kill people?"

When Schweitzer asked her what she meant, he was shocked at what he heard. During the six years of his absence, a sort of secret society made up of people who went around armed with leopards' paws and literally clawed their victims to death had developed. Fear and corruption had promoted the spread of the sect, and it had reached truly worrying proportions. The only way to fight it was to educate the Africans, removing them from their ignorance and poverty.

# The Epidemic

However, the hospital was about to undergo another even more terrifying trial. An epidemic of a form of dysentery that was unfamiliar to the doctors had broken out. The medicines at the hospital were ineffective and the epidemic soon threatened to assume gigantic proportions. When the first contagious cases arrived at the hospital, Schweitzer tried to organize an isolation ward. He wanted to avoid contact between these cases and the other patients, since a dysentery epidemic called for a very careful observance of the rules of hygiene. The most difficult thing was to persuade the Africans to avoid anything that could spread the disease—touching the infected or the objects they had touched, and above all, never drinking unboiled water. The most dangerous source of contamination was the river, since it was quite possible that dysentery cases washed in it several miles upstream.

These were terrible days, and even Schweitzer seemed to lose heart sometimes. One day he had had enough.

"What a fool I was to come to this country and try to look after these ignorant people."

Joseph was nearby, and answered quickly.

"You might seem an idiot on earth, but not in heaven."

Once they had gotten over the peak of the epidemic, it was time to take stock of its consequences. It had killed most of the able-bodied men. Many children and even entire families were left abandoned and were now starving to death. The hospital could never hope to feed all those extra mouths.

Schweitzer asked the authorities for help, and sent urgent requests to Europe.

"There is an entire population here dying of starvation for want of a handful of rice. They need immediate assistance; not a minute must be lost."

The motor launch which the Swedish section of the "Friends" had donated to the hospital proved invaluable. Loaded to the gunwales with provisions, it saved the lives of thousands of people who lived too far away in the jungle to come and seek help for themselves.

One way to halt the spread of the disease was to stop the overcrowding at the hospital by building a new one nearby. At the same time, new arable land would be won from the jungle. But a new site had to be chosen and Schweitzer knew of a spot only two miles upstream. However, it would take a year to get the first buildings erected and the enterprise would probably take an enormous amount of effort. Would it be worth it? After a long meeting, Schweitzer and his other colleagues from Europe decided that it would, and immediately got down to making preparations for the arduous enterprise. Various people in Europe had listened to Schweitzer's messages and appeals, and the hospital now had a permanent staff of three doctors and two nurses.

The meeting that evening lasted a long time because the doctor wanted his colleagues to know of all the data he had collected on the epidemic so that they

would realize how serious the situation was. All of them realized the difficulty of the task they were taking on, but they were also certain that there was no other way of dealing with the overcrowding. Quickly, permission to start building was requested and granted.

As he had done years before when building the first hospital, Schweitzer formed as many gangs of workmen as he could. He asked relatives of his patients to pay for the services they had received from the hospital by putting in a few hours of work. He also asked for help in Europe, with the result that sometime later an expert carpenter arrived from France. His contribution was to be decisive. The work had to go ahead at a furious pace, and a huge area of forest had to be cleared, so that at least a part of the hospital would be ready almost immediately for the isolation of dysentery cases. While the hospital was being built, Schweitzer and his colleagues often worked as carpenters themselves so that the work could proceed more rapidly. The workmen were often put off by the size of the job, but the encouraging presence of Schweitzer working among them helped the job along marvelously.

Almost a year had passed since they had decided to build the new hospital and on the morning of January 21, 1927, the first patients were moved to the new buildings. The whole river celebrated the occasion. Anyone who had a boat, a launch, or a canoe had lent it to the hospital for the move. The patients were spellbound at their first sight of the new hospital. All the buildings had been constructed on piles to keep out the snakes and allow flood water to flow under the buildings without carrying them away during the rainy season. They were all aligned from east to west so as to keep direct sun out of the wards, and the solid metal roofs kept out the sun as well as the rain. The infectious cases ward was in a separate building apart from the others. All dysentery cases were taken there at once, and this real isolation contributed more than just a little to halting the spread of the disease.

# The Hospital in the Jungle

The first days in the new hospital were like one long holiday—it seemed impossible that they were all working in such a comfortable, and above all, permanent place. The future of the hospital now seemed assured. More and more doctors and nurses were coming from Europe to devote two or three years of their lives to the sick of Lambaréné.

Feeling that the hospital could go on well enough without him for a time, Schweitzer decided to spend a year in Europe with his wife and daughter. He also needed medical treatment, for disease was affecting his health quite seriously and

he had had a second attack of malaria which had weakened him considerably.

When he was completely well again, Schweitzer left with Hélène for Lambaréné at Christmas, 1930. When Hélène saw the hospital after her absence of thirteen years, she was overwhelmed by the changes that had occurred since the chicken coop back in the old days.

The dysentery epidemic had been completely stamped out, the isolation ward was practically empty, and everything seemed to point to a more or less tranquil future. By now, the Schweitzers' life was there at Lambaréné, and their family had become as big as the hospital itself.

The fame of the hospital had spread far and wide during the years, and there was a continuous stream of visitors eager to see the "hospital in the jungle".

Meanwhile, the world was preparing for another, even more terrible war than the last one. Schweitzer wrote and sent messages all over the world asking for peace and brotherhood among humans.

As time passed, Schweitzer was increasingly obliged to reduce his activity at the hospital. He was old now and could no longer perform operations, but he never once thought of returning to Europe— his life would have no meaning away from Lambaréné. His greatest consolation was simply the fact that now his contribution was no longer needed. Many doctors came to Lambaréné and others had followed his example in other places—the hospital on the Ogowe was no longer a lucky rarity. Hospitals and leper colonies were now springing up throughout many parts of Africa as a result of his pioneering efforts at Lambaréné.

The hospital now had the clean, efficient look of a proper hospital, and might have been located in any European city. The operating room was very well equipped thanks to donations of money and equipment from Europe. The isolation ward worked properly now, allowing potentially contagious cases to be kept separate from other patients, reducing the risk of epidemics. There was even a separate section for the treatment of the dreaded sleeping sickness.

Near the hospital Schweitzer had a stockade in which he kept animals from the jungle. He had a deep respect for all forms of life, including plants and animals. Any creature in need found refuge at Lambaréné, and so the hospital had opened a special section for antelopes, cats, parrots, and all types of animals. The doctor could often be found walking around among the hospital buildings followed by his animals.

In the spare time he had after performing his hospital duties, Schweitzer busied himself with writing. He had experienced much during his long stay in Africa, and now he wanted to relate it to others so that his work would be known and more people would be willing to give part of their lives, or even just part of their income, to people whose only fault was to have been born in countries ignored by everyone.

All his time in Africa had done nothing to lessen his love for the music of Bach and his theological studies. In his final years at Lambaréné he at last found time to finish all the work he had begun, and to develop still further his already marvelous skill as an organist.

The people of Gabon were continually coming to the hospital. The medical team of four doctors and three nurses had even managed to provide a regular out-patient service. As they traveled around the villages, the doctors were able to see which diseases were spreading, and vaccinate all the inhabitants in the area.

But if people came to the hospital, it was because they had faith in Schweitzer. In the remote villages it was always "Doctor Schweitzer's Hospital" that they spoke of, and the sick wanted to be treated only by the white doctor. However, he did no more examinations personally, except in special cases. He followed hospital routine and advised the other doctors, but he no longer kept office hours or made rounds.

The day came, nevertheless, when his skill was once again indispensable. A young child had been found in extremely serious condition, but none of the doctors could diagnose the disease. When the case had been declared hopeless, the parents insisted that Schweitzer see the child. Thanks to his long experience, he was able to diagnose the disease after performing a thorough examination. Once again he saved a life.

# Two Graves Covered with Flowers

Schweitzer was awarded the Nobel Peace Prize in 1952. Only seven years had passed since the end of the Second World War, and he had been a living example of how people can help one another, irrespective of racial, religious, or geographical differences. From then on there was an unending stream of honors, prizes, and degrees—the world came to know more and more of Lambaréné and its doctor. Albert Einstein met Schweitzer on one of his visits to the United States and described him as "the greatest man alive".

Schweitzer died on September 4, 1965 at the age of ninety, surrounded by the children, patients, and animals he had devoted his life to curing from illness. He was laid to rest near Hélène, who had died in 1957, in the small cemetery at Lambaréné.

If you ever go there, you will recognize their graves immediately by the mounds of flowers covering them. You will also see a long procession of Africans paying homage at the grave of a man who was their first sign of love and hope in a hostile world.

# GABON

**History:** In the pre-colonial era, the territory that now makes up the Republic of Gabon was inhabited by Bantu peoples. It is not known exactly when they came to that area. Portuguese sailors reached the coast of Gabon in the 15th century. The Dutch, French, and English followed quickly in their wake. The goal of all the colonial powers was to make the country a reserve for the slave trade. In the first half of the 19th century, Gabon came under French control. As a result of a recently signed international agreement, the French had the task of stamping out the slave trade. Thus, Gabon became a French colony.

In 1849 the slave ship "Elisia" was captured by the French. A large number of liberated slaves founded, on a natural inlet on the coast, the city which was later to become the capital, Libreville. Other slaves, captured at sea, gradually increased the population. Gabon gained its independence in 1960, when the Independent Republic of Gabon was proclaimed, and developed its own constitution and governmental system. At present its main cities and populations are the capital, Libreville (186,000), Port Gentil (85,000), Lambaréné (23,000), Tehibauga (21,000), Mouila (20,000), Franceville (16,000), Oyem (16,000) and Koulamoutou (10,000).

**Borders:** The coast line of Gabon is 500 miles long. It fronts on the South Atlantic Ocean. To the north the country borders on Equatorial Guinea and the Cameroons, and to the east and south with the People's Republic of the Congo.

**Religion:** Over half the population has been converted to Christianity. Gabon now has the highest Christian population of all the countries which once comprised French Equatorial Africa. Apart from Protestant and Islamic minorities, the rest of the inhabitants follow traditional African religions.

The capital of Gabon stands on the estuary of the River Gabon. It was named Libreville because it was founded by freed slaves.

Schweitzer's hospital on the River Ogowe.

# SCHWEITZER AND COLONIALISM

Once the First World War had ended and while Schweitzer was in Europe in 1917, he began writing a book describing his life in Africa. Entitled *On the Edge of the Primeval Forest* it quickly became enormously popular. His account of his life in Africa gave him the chance to express his opinions on the many serious problems of colonialism. A few extracts will help us to understand his thinking on the matter. (Remember that these are the words of a man writing early in the twentieth century.)

*"Do we whites have the right to impose our laws on primitive and semi-primitive peoples—the only ones I have had personal experience of? If we simply want to dominate them and exploit the material wealth of their countries, the answer is no. If we really want to educate them and help them to achieve a decent standard of living, then the answer is yes.*

*"Unfortunately, many of those who have occupied colonial territories in our name have only equalled the original chiefs in cruelty, violence, and injustice, and have burdened all of us with a great guilt and shame. The iniquities which, even today, are being perpetrated on native populations can be neither ignored nor excused. However, to concede an independence to primitive and semi-primitive populations which for them would simply mean slavery under one or another of their own chiefs is no way to put right the wrongs we have committed. The only way is to exercise the power we really do possess to the advantage of the natives, thereby justifying to them morally the very fact that we possess it. Even 'imperialism' can claim to have a certain moral value for the good. It has ended the slave trade and has put an end to the incessant wars between the native peoples which were a common feature of the past, creating long-lasting peace over huge areas of the globe.*

*"The tragic thing is that the interests of colonialism and civilization do not always coincide, and are, indeed, often directly in conflict with each other. The best thing for the native peoples would be for them to progress from a nomadic or semi-nomadic existence to being farmers and sedentary craftsmen, under a wise government which is as little as possible concerned with commercial interests."*

From Albert Schweitzer, <u>My Life and Thought</u>

A village on the way to Lambaréné.

A photograph of Doctor Schweitzer.

# SCHWEITZER AND PEACE

On the 28th, 29th, and 30th of April, 1958, Albert Schweitzer, winner of the Nobel Peace Prize in 1952, broadcast three appeals on Radio Oslo against the threat of nuclear warfare. This had already become a major threat to the continuing existence of humankind. The extracts that follow are taken from his appeal on April 29. As can be seen, the message is still important for anyone who wishes to pay attention to it.

*"We are now faced with the frightening prospect of a nuclear war between the Soviet Union and the United States. This can be avoided only if the nuclear powers decide, of their own common accord, to ban their nuclear weapons...*

*"There is another reason why we should expect the situation to get worse. America now supplies nuclear weapons to other countries, assuming that they will not be rash or irresponsible in their use of them. Clearly, the other two nuclear powers can do the same. Who can guarantee that, among these favored peoples, there are not some who will make what use they want of the weapons, without thinking of the consequences for others? Who can stop them? Who can persuade them not to use their nuclear weapons, even if other peoples are wiser and agree not to use theirs? A small crack has appeared in the dyke, and we should watch now to see that it is not swept away...*

*"From whatever point of view we regard the issue, the danger of nuclear war is so great that it is absolutely imperative to abolish nuclear weapons. The theory that peace can be maintained only by intimidating other countries with the weapons they do not possess is no longer valid today, now that the danger of war is such a real one..."*

From Albert Schweitzer, <u>The People Must Know</u>

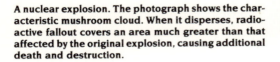

**A nuclear explosion. The photograph shows the characteristic mushroom cloud. When it disperses, radioactive fallout covers an area much greater than that affected by the original explosion, causing additional death and destruction.**

# THE MUSIC OF BACH

The following is a passage about Bach written by Schweitzer. It helps us to understand Schweitzer's profound feeling for music.

"...In my book I advance the claims of Bach the painter and poet over and against those of Bach the composer of 'pure music'. He wanted to reproduce in sound with the maximum clarity and fidelity what he found in the written text, whether it was sentimental or figurative. Above all, he tried to trace images in sound. He is more of a painter than a poet...

"If the text speaks of thick swirling fogs, raging winds, rivers in full spate, the sea swells, falling leaves, tolling bells, well-tried faith that strides ahead, hesitant faith that barely manages to inch forward, the fall of the proud, the rise of Satan or the angels—all of these things can be seen and heard in his music. Bach, in fact, has a true musical language. He uses recurring rhythmic motifs of serene beatitude, intense joy, violent grief and sublime pain. The impulse to express poetic and figurative thought is the essence of the music, which is directed at the creative imagination of the listener and attempts to recreate in him the sensations and visions from which the music was originally created. This can only happen when someone has the mysterious ability to reproduce thought with a directness and clarity that goes beyond its intrinsic expressive capacities. In this, Bach was the greatest of the great. His music is poetic and pictorial because his themes are triggered off by poetic and pictorial images. From these images, the music develops into a complete edifice in sound; essentially poetic and pictorial music is presented as a Gothic artifice in sound. The main feature of this art is the spirituality which emanates from its wonderfully vital, astoundingly plastic and formally perfect textures."

From Albert Schweitzer, <u>My Life and Thought</u>

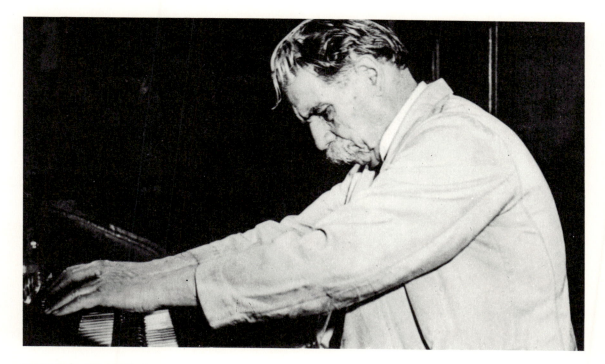

**Doctor Schweitzer at the organ.**

**Mycenae—the city walls with the Lion Gate.**

# Historical Chronology

| The Life of Schweitzer | Historical and Cultural Events |
|---|---|
| **1875** Born at Kayserberg in Alsace, the son of a Protestant minister. The family moves to Gunsbach, where Albert was to spend his childhood. | **1874** Schliemann excavates Mycenae.<br><br>Bell and Gray begin producing telephones on an industrial scale. |
| | **1878** Thomas Edison invents the phonograph. |
| | **1879** Edison produces the first electric light bulb. |
| | **1881** Opening of the St. Gothard Tunnel. Siemens builds the first electric tram.<br><br>Pablo Picasso is born at Malaga. He will become one of the greatest painters of this century. |
| | **1882** The founding of the Triple Alliance between Germany, Austria, and Italy. |
| | **1885** Benz and Daimler build an automobile with an internal combustion engine. |
| | **1889** The Eiffel Tower is built for the Universal Exhibition at Paris. |
| **1893** Studies the organ in Paris and enrolls in the Faculty of Theology and Philosophy at Strasbourg University. | **1893** Diesel produces his motor. |

**Thomas Edison's original phonograph.**

**Pablo Picasso—Family of Acrobats with a Monkey.**

**The Eiffel Tower, Paris, built for the Universal Exhibition.**

| The Life of Schweitzer | Historical and Cultural Events | |
|---|---|---|
| | **1894** | Alfred Dreyfus, the French colonel, is condemned for treason. The sentence was to be annulled in 1906 and Dreyfus released. |
| | **1895-1896** | Japan wins a decisive victory over China and is assured the possession of Formosa. |
| | **1897** | Marconi invents the wireless telephone. |
| **1899** He is curate and preacher at the church of St. Nicholas in Strasbourg. | **1899** | The first FIAT car is produced in Italy. |
| **1904** Already famous as an organist and theologian, he decides to study medicine in order to go to Gabon and look after the natives there. | **1903** | The Wright brothers make the first piloted flight in an engined aircraft. |
| **1905** Studies medicine at Strasbourg University. | **1905** | The first Russian Revolution breaks out, and is crushed with a mixture of concessions and repressive measures. Einstein explains the theory of relativity. |
| | **1909** | Discovery of north pole by Robert E. Peary. |
| **1911** Goes to Paris to specialize in tropical medicine. Marries Hélène Bresslau. | **1911** | The "Blaue Reiter" ("The Blue Knight") group of artists mounts its first joint exhibition. Kandinsky illustrates the cover of their almanac. |

The disgracing of Colonel Dreyfus—an illustration from the "Piccolo Giornale".

The first FIAT 3½ HP car, designed by Faccioli.

The Wright brothers' "Flying Machine" —the first piloted flight in an engined aircraft.

Wassily Kandinsky—sketch for the "Blue Knight" almanac.

| The Life of Schweitzer | Historical and Cultural Events |
|---|---|
| **1913** With Hélène, leaves for Gabon and starts work under trying conditions. | |
| **1914** Their work is interrupted by the outbreak of the First World War. | **1914** Archduke Franz Ferdinand of Austria is assassinated at Sarajevo. This leads to the outbreak of the First World War. |
| **1914-1918** They are deported to France as prisoners of war and interned in a concentration camp. As a result of an exchange of prisoners, they are released. | **1917** The "October Revolution" in Russia. The Commission of Commissariats takes power in the name of the proletariat. |
| | **1918** The First World War ends. Berlin rebels and the Kaiser abdicates. |
| **1919** Hélène has a daughter. | **1919** Benito Mussolini founds the Fascisti in Italy. Zapata, the revolutionary leader of Mexico and founder of its agrarian reforms, is assassinated. |
| **1924** After collecting funds with the aid of "The Friends of Lambaréné," Schweitzer returns alone to Gabon. He finds the hospital in ruins. | |

The assassination of Archduke Franz Ferdinand of Austria, from 'La Domenica del Corriere'.

A French Ministry of Agriculture poster of the First World War.

The Kremlin, Moscow. A fortress of the Czars since 1500, it became the seat of Soviet Government in 1918.

Emil Zapata, peasant leader of Mexico and founder of its agrarian reforms.

| The Life of Schweitzer | | Historical and Cultural Events | |
|---|---|---|---|
| **1925** | A new hospital is built with the help of Africans and Europeans. | **1925** | Mussolini announces the start of a true dictatorship. |
| | | **1926** | Grazia Deledda wins the Nobel Prize for Literature. |
| **1927** | The new hospital opens. | **1928** | The first "talkie", "The Jazz Singer", is produced in the United States. |
| **1929** | Schweitzer is reunited with his wife. | **1929** | The Wall Street Crash leads to the Great Depression in the United States. |
| **1930** | They return to Lambaréné. | **1934** | Hitler unites the offices of Chancellor and President of the Reich, after obtaining a popular mandate and eliminating his opponents in Germany. |
| | | **1936-1939** | Stalin's "Great Purges" in Russia eliminate his political opponents. |
| | | **1939** | Outbreak of the Second World War, involving the major world powers. |
| **1952** | Schweitzer is awarded the Nobel Peace Prize. | **1945** | Japan surrenders to the United States after the atomic bomb is dropped on two Japanese cities. The Second World War ends. |
| **1965** | Dies on September 4th at Lambaréné, aged ninety. | | |

Benito Mussolini—a photo-portrait of the Italian leader.

The New York Stock Exchange after the crash. Worthless shares are scattered on the floor.

Berlin—the Brandenburg Gate decorated with the Swastika.

A nuclear explosion, showing the characteristic mushroom cloud.

# Further Reading

Brabazon, James. *Albert Schweitzer, A Biography*. New York: G.P. Putnam's Sons, 1975.
Franck, Frederick. *Days with Albert Schweitzer—The Story of His Life*. New York: Holt, Rinehart, & Winston, 1959.
Schweitzer, Albert. *On the Edge of the Primeval Forest*. tr. by C.T. Campion. New York: Macmillan, 1948.

# Index

2 3 4 5 6 7 8 9 10—IL—93 92 91 90 89 88 87 86